Crafts for Christmas

Also by Katherine N. Cutler

Growing a Garden Indoors or Out

Creative Shellcraft

From Petals to Pinecones:
A Nature Art and Craft Book

CRAFTS
FOR
CHRISTMAS

by

Katherine N. Cutler
and Kate Cutler Bogle

illustrated by Jacqueline Adato

Lothrop, Lee & Shepard Company / New York

We are grateful to many of our friends for sharing some of their ideas with us, but particularly to our sister and aunt, Virginia Pelton. Our thanks go also to our ever patient husbands, Westy and David.

2   3   4   5   78   77   76   75

Library of Congress Cataloging in Publication Data

Cutler, Katherine N.
    Crafts for Christmas.

    SUMMARY: Instructions for making nearly fifty gifts, decorations, and foods for Christmas using natural materials and discardable miscellaneous items.
    1. Christmas decorations—Juvenile literature. 2. Christmas cookery—Juvenile literature. 3. Gifts—Juvenile literature. [1. Christmas decorations. 2. Christmas cookery. 3. Gifts] I. Bogle, Kate Cutler, joint author. II. Adato, Jacqueline, illus. III. Title.
TT900.C4C87   745.59'41   74-8750
ISBN 0-688-41663-2   ISBN 0-688-51663-7 (lib. bdg.)

Contents

1912059

Introduction

Most of us think of Christmas as a festival to celebrate the birth of Christ—and indeed it is. But long before Christ was born primitive people who worshiped the sun held a celebration at this time of the year to mark the Winter Solstice, the time that the sun started its course back toward earth from the farthest place from the equator.

The pagans used evergreen garlands and wreaths for their celebration of the Solstice. They believed that the round wreath was a symbol of eternity, and evergreen branches a symbol of eternal life. Holly, ivy and mistletoe were used because they are not only green in winter, but bear fruit then as well.

The Christmas tree, as we know it, is an outgrowth of the ancient kissing bough, a garland or branch of green, often mistletoe, from which small presents hung on long ribbons. It became a tradition that a maiden caught standing beneath the mistletoe bough could be kissed.

The Christians incorporated many of these pagan customs with those they associated with Christ's birth—the giving of gifts, creches and carols, stars and angels. Through the years they have also adopted Christmas customs from other lands—lighting candles at Christmas from Scandinavian countries, carol singing from Germany and Yule logs and plum pudding from England.

All of these traditions combined make Christmas one of the gayest and merriest times of the year. But we should not forget the deeper spiritual meaning of the holiday. Christmas is also a time of sharing and remembering. A time when it is fun to make gifts for our families and neighbors, or send a card to a distant friend.

In this book we are sharing with you some of the things we have enjoyed making at Christmas in the hope that you will enjoy making them too.

While we will give specific directions for individual projects, there are certain fundamental supplies that are convenient to have on hand when you make Christmas decorations. These include:

assorted decorations—beads, sequins, pieces of ribbon, yarn, raffia, glitter and any other odds and ends you may have collected during the year.

florist picks—pointed wooden sticks wired at one end. These can be purchased at a florist shop.

glue—a glue that is non-toxic, non-flammable and transparent when it dries is most satisfactory. Sobo, Elmer's, Formica and Borden's are glues which are very adhesive and are water soluble.

heavy shears

scissors

wire—spools of wire are numbered according to thickness. Lower numbers are for heavy wire and the higher numbers, the finer wire. Numbers 18, 19, and 20 are useful for the projects described in this book.

Decorations and Gifts from Natural Materials

There is really nothing as beautiful as real plant material for making Christmas decorations. Nothing can substitute for the rich green color and the fragrance of pine boughs. Branches of holly with shiny green leaves and bright red berries bring the spirit of Christmas to everyone. In spite of the cold and snow, woods and fields of the Northeast and parts of the Midwest are full of greens and berries that can be gathered. We will discuss them in describing how to make wreaths.

The South and West have different, but no less attractive plants to use for Christmas decorations. There is feathery green podocarpus, pittosporum with clusters of green rosettes, various palms, red and green croton leaves, hibiscus, and of course the beautiful Christmas flower, poinsettia. Red hibiscus flowers are beautiful against a background of podocarpus. The blossoms last only a day, but they will last for that day out of water, so that you can place them anywhere among the greens. Or you can make a large bouquet of them by spearing the blossoms on the ends of the long pliant spines of coconut fronds.

Another gay Christmas arrangement can be made by painting the rosettes of pittosporum red, and using them as blossoms with other greens.

Fruit is most attractive when it is sprayed gold to empha-

9

size the texture of its skin. For instance, the grainy surfaces of tangerines, oranges, and kumquats make a fascinating contrast to the smooth appearance of grapes, pears and apples. It is also pleasing to arrange the gold fruit with limes and avocados in their natural green state.

There are many things in nature to look for to provide material for making Christmas gifts and decorations. Some of these are:

Cones	*Seedpods*	*Weeds*
Balsam	Catalpa	Cattails
Blackpine	Cotton	Dock
Casuarina	Eucalyptus	Evening Primrose
Deodar	Iris	Goldenrod (dry)
Hemlock	Jacaranda	Queen Anne's lace (dry)
Pinyon-pine	Locust	Sea Grass
Redwood	Lotus	Yarrow (dry)
Sequoia	Mallow	
Spruce	Milkweed	
	Okra	
	Sweet Gum	
	Wisteria	
	Yucca	

However, there are some plants that need protection because they are not in plentiful supply. Also there are plants like ground pine that take several years to mature, and when the running roots are carelessly torn up it is not long before the plant disappears. Therefore, before you start gathering plant material it would be wise to get a list of plants that should be protected in your area from your county agricultural agent or state garden club.

You can use your material in its natural state or spray it gold or silver. Like fruit, when it is sprayed the difference in various textures is attractively emphasized.

Preserved foliage is beautiful to use with dried or sprayed material. To have it, though, you must start long before Christmas because you must gather branches before the leaves have begun to dry.

To preserve foliage, stand the branches of leaves in a solution made from one-third glycerin and two-thirds water. The liquid should be about five inches deep. Crush or slit the stems so that there will be more area to absorb the solution. The preserving will be complete when small beads of moisture appear on the leaves. This will take from a few days to two or more weeks, depending on the material. The leaves will change color—usually to a shade of brown, and will be like supple leather. You can use them indefinitely, and in many ways.

Use little bunches as wreath decorations.

Tie a cluster in the bow of a Christmas package.

Spray some of the weeds silver, and while they are wet dust them with glitter. Fill a tunafish can (with the label removed) with styrofoam and make an arrangement of the sparkling weeds in it.

Paint three empty pillboxes of graduated sizes gold. Glue them close together on a wooden wall plaque and fill them with dried material in an attractive arrangement.

Substitute some of the sprayed material for the artificial holly in the doorstop described on page 55.

Wreaths

Because Christmas wreaths can be made from many different things, part of the fun is gathering materials for them. You may cut greens in snowy woods, gather shells on a sunny beach or collect dried weeds and seedpods from the fields on a crisp fall day.

Probably the wreath that we think of as most basic is one made from evergreens.

You Will Need:
pruning shears
pieces of evergreen
a foundation hoop
spool of wire

The foundation of such a wreath is a firm foundation hoop. One way of making this is to cut a pliable wand from a willow tree or a cane from a bush such as privet or forsythia, at least four feet long, and as thick as a lead pencil. Strip the leaves.

Hold the cane at its thickest end, and make a circle the size you wish. (Remember that the wreath will be larger

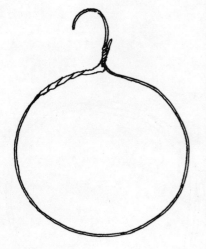

when you add the evergreen material). Reinforce the circle by twisting the remainder of the cane over and around the circle until you use it all. Fasten the end securely by weaving it into the twists of the circle. Attach a wire loop for hanging.

Another way to make a foundation hoop is to bend a coat hanger into a circle, leaving the hook at the top to hang it by. When you use this method, wrap the wire with masking tape to make a less slippery surface.

Cut pieces of evergreen three or more inches long, depending on the size of the wreath. Avoid using those whose needles drop readily like hemlock and cedrus atlantica.

Satisfactory greens to use are:
arborvitae
cedar
holly
juniper
laurel
rhododendron
spruce
yew

14

Wire the pieces in little bunches, thick enough to hide the frame but not so thick as to be cumbersome.

Fasten the end of a spool of wire to the top of the hoop. Hold a bunch of evergreens in place with one hand, and with the other wind the spool of wire over and around the hoop four or five times, covering an inch of the bunch at its base. Continue overlapping and winding the bunches with the spool of wire until the circle is covered.

You can make these wreaths well in advance of Christmas. Put them in a plastic bag and keep them in a cool place; outdoors in the snow, or even in the freezer.

Your imagination is the only limit for ways to decorate the wreaths. They are lovely just as they are with the addition of a stunning big bow. If the wreath is to be hung outside, though, be sure and use waterproof ribbon.

To make a bow for a wreath, make several wide loops of ribbon. Cut a piece of wire long enough to wrap tightly around the center of the loops, leaving a long end. When you have

wound the wire tightly several times around the center of the loops, twist and pull the loops each side of the center into a full bow shape. Wire it to the wreath with the long end of the center wire.

You can make a different kind of bow by cutting the shape from palmetto palm and spraying it gold or silver. Or you can soak corn husks until they are pliable, form them into a large bow and spray them also.

Cones, either in their natural state, or sprayed silver or gold are a favorite addition to wreaths, as they come in so many shapes and sizes. When you use a cone on a wreath, wedge wire under the petals at the base, and wind it around several times. Either leave a long end of wire to fasten it to the wreath, or wire the cone on a florist pick and thrust the wooden end of the pick into the greens. You can cut cones with tight, solidly-packed petals in half which gives the effect of a many petaled flower like a gardenia.

Sprays of berries make beautiful additions. Some of these are red holly,

16

nandina, multiflora rose and photinia, gray bayberry and juniper.

Fruit is also a favorite decoration. If fresh fruit is sprayed with shellac it will last well indoors, and even outdoors except in very severe weather. Fruits sprayed silver or gold are not only beautiful, but also last well. Those suitable for decorating wreaths are:

apples (small)
cranberries
grapes
kumquats
lady apples
lemons
limes
mandarins
seckel pears
tangerines

To fasten fruit to a wreath, push a fifteen inch piece of wire through the middle of the fruit and twist the ends together in the back. Use the twisted ends to wire it to the wreath. If the fruit has a stem, you can wire a florist pick to the stem and thrust the pointed end of the pick into the wreath.

17

Other decorations that are attractive
are:
artificial red birds
bells
candy canes
sleigh bells
small toys

Seedpod and Nut Wreath

Wreaths that we love to make are seed-pod wreaths. All year we collect cones of different shapes and sizes, nuts, coconut calyxes, and all sorts of fascinating seedpods, wood roses and dried weeds to use for this kind of wreath. It will surprise you how many interesting things you can find yourself.

To make this kind of a wreath you will need, besides the things mentioned above:

a wide circle of Masonite, wallboard or
    similar material
a can of linoleum paste
a putty knife

Assemble the dried materials on a sheet of newspaper. Fasten a wire loop around the top of the circle. With the putty knife spread linoleum paste over the circle thickly enough so that you can press the dried objects in it.

Now make a finished edge around the inner and outer parts of the circle. Use casuarina cones, almonds with the pointed ends out, or the individual petals of large cones to give a scalloped effect. (If these large cones don't grow near you, you can buy one or two at a florist. You can cut a quantity of petals from one cone.)

When you complete the borders, make focal points at the top and bottom of the wreath with a grouping of material. Use some of the larger interesting shapes for this like wood roses, cut cones or coconut calyxes. Next make smaller centers of interest on each side of the circle. Then to lead your eye around the circle use curved cones or pods between the centers of interest. This makes a basic design, and you can fill in the rest of the space solidly with the rest of the material. Be sure to use plenty of paste, so that everything stays in place. It takes several hours for the paste to get completely hard, but this is good, for if you want to make some changes in the design after you complete the wreath you can.

You can either leave the wreath in its natural shades of brown, or spray it silver or gold. One of these wreaths is very effective wired in the center of a green one. To do this put the pod wreath flat on a larger green one, centers together. Wire them together at the top, sides, and bottom by winding pieces of strong wire around both wreaths, concealing it between the seed-pods and under the greens.

Shell Wreath

If you live near the seashore, it is fun to make a shell wreath in the same way that you do the seedpod one. Miniature clam, mussel or coquina shells are good to use for the borders, and the wealth of shapes and sizes of other shells lend themselves for a most interesting design. You can leave the shells in their natural colors, or spray them silver or gold to show an interesting variety of texture. These wreaths, too, are lovely against a green one.

Asparagus Sprengeri Wreath

Asparagus Sprengeri fern, which grows profusely in warm climates, makes lovely Christmas wreaths. The small feathery leaves grow on long pliant stems that are easy to bind together in a wreath shape. To make it full, wire several circles together. An effective way to decorate such a wreath is to fasten wire to real or artificial clusters of red berries, and thrust the end of the wire into the center of green pittosporum rosettes.

Or you can wire green and red croton leaves in bow-like clusters.

Bough for Displaying Christmas Cards

You Will Need:
a large bare branch
gold spray paint
needlepoint flower holder
piece of hardware cloth
sprays of evergreen

It is fun to display Christmas cards as they arrive, but often there are so many the effect is overwhelming. Why not be selective? You can feature one category in this way.

Select a large bare branch with interesting curved side branches. Spray it gold. Attach tiny Christmas balls to the tips of each branch. Then as cards arrive, tie all those that fit one category on the branches with gold cord. You might feature Santa Clauses, Christmas trees, holly and mistletoe, etc.

In our house we use a large bough from a Japanese pine with cones attached, and hang on it all the cards we receive that feature birds.

There is an easy way to make a large

branch stand firmly upright. Choose a heavy needlepoint holder like those used in flower arranging. Cut a piece of hardware cloth (the heavy quarter-inch mesh that you buy in a hardware store) the proper size to wrap around the bottom three inches of the bough, allowing an extra inch to extend beyond the end. Nail it to the bough. Thrust the extended end of the hardware cloth into the sharp pins of the holder, and the bough will stand upright. Arrange pieces of evergreen around the base of the bough, concealing the needlepoint holder and the hardware cloth.

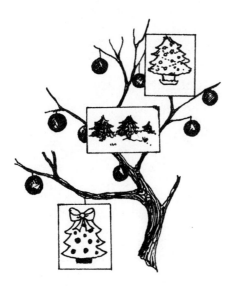

Pine Cone and Nut Tree

Sometimes there is a place for a Christmas decoration that is not red or green or shiny and glittering. One that fits this category is a cone and nut Christmas tree.

You Will Need:
a large cone with open petals
some mixed nuts in the shell
a block of wood
glue
shellac

Glue the cone to the block of wood which acts as a base. Dip the tip of a nut into glue, and insert it between the petals of the cone. Repeat this, varying the nuts until all the spaces are filled. Use larger nuts toward the bottom, and smaller ones toward the top. When everything is in place spray the entire tree with clear varnish. This will give it a pretty finish, and help to preserve it. Such a tree lasts indefinitely.

26

Woodland Christmas Tree

If you live near woods where you can choose and cut your own Christmas tree you can also have the fun of making decorations for it from natural things.

A family that we know had one of the loveliest trees we've ever seen, and the only things that they bought for it were gold tinsel roping and strings of tiny natural lights. For ornaments they gathered pine cones, nuts, sweet gum balls, seedpods, and sprays of berries and sprayed them all gold. When the tree was garlanded with the roping and the lights, and the golden ornaments were hung in place, the effect was breathtaking.

Clamshell Creche

You Will Need:
a large surf clamshell
some small, very thin pieces of
  driftwood
glue
a small, dried starfish
tiny creche figures
piece of gold cord

There is a Christmas-tree ornament
made from a clamshell that is a favorite
in our family. This handsome ornament
is a clamshell creche.

Some clamshells have a mottled dark lining that looks like a cloudy night sky. When we make this ornament, we try to find one of these. Drill two small holes at the top of the shell, and thread the cord through them and tie a knot to make a loop for hanging.

Now you will need some small, very thin pieces of driftwood. To clean them and make them look satiny, rub two pieces together.

Build a miniature shelter inside the clamshell with the pieces of driftwood this way. Choose one piece a little wider than the others and long enough to reach within an inch of the shell edges. This will be the floor of the shelter. Hold this at right angles to the shell near the bottom and cover the edge that touches the shell with glue. Now you will need a lot of patience, because you will have to hold the driftwood to the shell until the glue adheres, and you think it will *never* stick. But believe it or not, it finally will, and will remain firm.

Now with other small pieces make the side walls, gluing the edges to the floor and to the shell. Again, be patient. When the floor and side walls are in place, find a piece to go across the top for a roof. If this has a slight curve it is more interesting. It doesn't matter if the roof isn't solidly closed, as this is supposed to be a crude shelter.

At many arts-and-crafts and variety stores you can buy tiny creche figures. Glue these to the floor. As a finishing touch glue a starfish to the hinge of the shell. The dark nightlike background of the shell, the crude shelter, and the simple figures inside the shelter combine to make an effective nativity scene.

Shell Magnets

You Will Need:
small shells
small magnets
glue
plastic bags and ribbon for packaging

Many of you are familiar with magnets in the form of fruits or vegetables used to pin notes to a metal surface in the kitchen. More unusual ones are made from natural shells.

You can buy small magnets, round or oblong, in hobby shops. These will fit, reinforced by a little glue, into the openings of shells. All you have to do is to select shells that have the appropriate openings and glue the magnets in place.

A few of these, prettily packaged, make an attractive and practical gift.

Shell Fish Ornament

You Will Need:
both sides of a rounded shell
heavy foil
glue
wire or cord
2 small shells

Cut three curved fins from the foil, leaving the bottom side square. Put glue on each side of the shell at the joint where they were hinged. Put glue on the square bottom of the fins, and on the ends of the cord or wire (which will form the hanging loop). Insert the glued ends of the fins at three points between the rounded edge of the shell. Also insert the cord or wire. Press the edges of the shell together over the inserted objects until the glue sets. This may take as much as five minutes. Glue two small shells at the joint for eyes.

Walnut Tree Ornament

You Will Need:
walnuts
cord
glue
gold or silver spray paint

You can make very pretty ornaments for the Christmas tree with walnuts. Insert a blunt knife into the crack in a walnut, and pry it apart, being careful to keep the two halves intact. Remove the nutmeat to eat, or use in making candy or cookies.

Glue the halves of the nuts back together again with a loop of cord for hanging stuck between them. Spray them silver or gold. These ornaments will last well from year to year.

Package Wrappings
with Cones and Shells

You Will Need:
brown wrapping, or colored glazed
   paper
glue
heavy colored yarn
small pine cones or shells
wire

While gay ribbon-bedecked packages
are beautiful at Christmas, sometimes
something simpler is a nice change. To
make such a charming Christmas package, gild some small pine cones and
wire them in clusters. Wrap your box
in plain ordinary brown wrapping
paper. Tie it with green yarn ribbon,
and fasten the pine cone clusters to the
bow.

Solid color glazed papers make a
lovely background for packages decorated with shells. Glue small shells
similar in shape and size around the
edge for a border, and make a cluster of
larger shells to include in the ribbon
bow. Do this by drilling small holes in
the shells and wiring them together.

If you don't live where there are shells, you can get much the same effect by gilding small shell macaroni for the border and larger shell forms for the bow cluster.

Bayberry Bags

You Will Need:
bayberries
heavy cotton material

Early settlers in New England valued gray bayberries not only for their beauty, but for the wax that they contained. Many of their candles were made from the fragrant berries. This was a long and tedious process, because it took bushels of berries to get enough wax for a few candles.

However there is an easier project that has been handed down from generation to generation that we can make as welcome gifts today. Any housekeeper would cherish one—namely a pretty bag filled with bayberries to keep on the ironing board. When a hot iron is placed on the bag, wax from the berries comes through the covering and keeps the surface of the iron smooth.

If you live where bayberries grow, gather a quantity of them. Make a bag like a bean bag from some sturdy material like denim and fill the bag with enough berries to make it about half to three-quarters of an inch thick when lying flat. Double stitch it around the edges. For Christmas gifts you might want to make the bags in the shape of stars or bells.

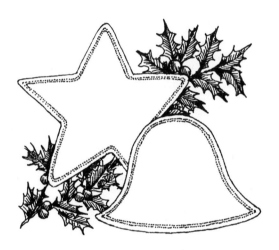

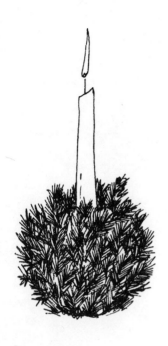

Apple Candle Holder

You Will Need:
a candle
a large red apple

Candles add greatly to Christmas festivities, especially if they are in pretty decorative holders. This is a holder that is effective and very easy to make.

Select a large red apple, being sure to choose one that is perfectly flat at the blossom end. This is so that it will stand upright. Make a hole in the stem end with an applecorer or a knife to fit the candle you are using. If you make the hole a little smaller at the bottom than at the top, the candle will dig into the pulp and stay firm when you push it into the apple.

Cut pieces of evergreen with small shiny leaves like boxwood or ilex, and insert them in the surface of the apple until it is covered, and has a completely rounded effect like a green ball. The juice in the apple will keep the greens fresh a long time.

Narcissus Bulb Gift

You Will Need:
paper white narcissus bulb
small bowl
small pebbles

A lovely gift at Christmas is a growing paper white narcissus. It takes three or four weeks for the bulb to bloom, so this gift must be planned ahead.

An empty margarine bowl makes an excellent container. You can leave it as is, or paint it. Use the top of a spray can as a base and fasten the bowl to it with modeling clay.

Put some pebbles in the bottom of the bowl. Place a paper white narcissus bulb on the pebbles, making sure to have the flat side down. Put more pebbles around the bulb to hold it firmly upright. Add water to the level of the bottom of the bulb.

Some people say that you should now put the bulb in a dark place until it sprouts, but we find that they do just as well where it is light.

Be sure to keep water at the level of the bottom of the bulb.

Decorations and Gifts Using Materials That are Ordinarily Discarded

Some of the materials that we ordinarily throw away can be useful in making Christmas gifts and decorations. Cans with separate plastic lids and bottles with wide-necked screw tops can become beautifully decorated containers for homemade goodies.

Margarine cups, foil or cardboard food containers, tin cans, used plastic glasses, spray can tops and plastic jugs are other materials that are included here, but there are many more that might offer a challenge to your originality.

Tart Pan Decoration

You Will Need:
foil tart cups
a styrofoam ball six or more inches in
    diameter
silver spray paint
silver glitter
green or red glitter
white-headed corsage pins
piece of firm wire
ribbon
glue

Save little foil tart cups from desserts, and you can use them to make a fascinating decoration. A young friend whose imagination has been fired by talk of unidentified flying objects refers to it as the U.F.O. ball. Hanging in a doorway, or from a center light, it is most attractive.

Thread the wire through the styrofoam ball and fasten it at one end with a hairpin loop, leaving enough at the other end to make a loop for hanging.

Spray the ball lightly with silver, rotating it on the wire spike.

41

Spread glue generously over the ball and cover with silver glitter for extra sparkle.

Coat the rims of the tart cups with glue and dip them in colored glitter. Paint the centers of the cups with glue, and also cover with colored glitter. Pin the cups to the ball by putting a corsage pin through the center of each into the ball, spacing them so that they cover the ball.

Wind the hanging loop with ribbon.

Using Foil Containers

You Will Need:
foil containers
cookie cutters in various shapes
enamel model paint
glue
pieces of felt
assorted glitter, sequins, beads, ribbon,
    etc.

At Christmas time you can make use of many of the foil containers that hold frozen foods or T. V. dinners to make tree ornaments, package decorations and place cards for holiday parties.

Cut the corners of the containers so that they lie flat. Place a cookie cutter on the foil and trace around it with a pencil. Cut out the shape, and decorate it.

For instance—trace and cut a star. Paint each side of it with glue and dip it in glitter. Make a hole in the top and attach a ribbon or cord to hang it to the tree. Or cut out a Santa Claus figure and paint in his red coat and cap, white beard and fur trimmed boots. Either of

43

these can be used as an ornament or package decoration.

To make a place card, when you cut out the figure leave an additional square piece at each side of the base and turn them back to make the figure stand. The one illustrated here is a tree. After you cut the foil shape, cut two similar ones from green felt. Glue them to the back and front of the foil. Cut a piece of cardboard to simulate a tiny package and write the name on the package. Cross red ribbons on the front of the tree, gluing the ends in back. Slip the name card under the crossed ribbons.

You can make a charming barnyard snow scene to put under the Christmas tree by cutting foil shapes or barnyard animals with cookie cutters, and painting them appropriately.

Spiral Foil Tree

A group of spiral foil trees of various sizes makes a very modern looking Christmas decoration. To make these trees is extremely simple.

Cut a circle of foil, and with kitchen shears start cutting a quarter of an inch from the edge and continue cutting around and around until you reach the center. Bend the end where you started and fasten it making a circle at the base.

Cut a star from a foil freezer container, paint it with glue, dip it in silver glitter, and fasten to top of tree.

Foil Angels

Aluminum foil freezer containers can be the basis for a little angel. In addition you will need only a tiny Christmas ball and a little glue.

Trace the pattern as shown. With kitchen shears cut along the dotted lines as shown in the diagram. Put a little piece of glue soaked cotton into the neck of a small Christmas ball, and stick the ball to the neck piece of the foil for a head. Fold the arms forward. Bend the halo in a circle to stand over

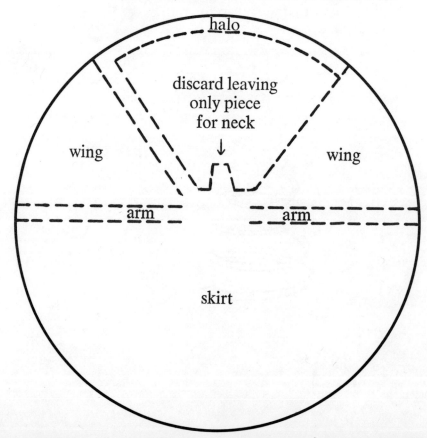

the head. Fold the skirt back so that the angel will stand.

For variation you can put glue on the wings and dip them in glitter. Or you can have the arms encircle a small bouquet of artificial flowers or gold and silver sprayed weeds.

These can be used as place cards, package ornaments, or hung on the tree. A group of them in front of a background of greens with some silver sprayed palmetto (which suggests a pipe organ) makes a pretty table decoration. In this case you can make folders of paper to glue on the arms for music books.

Christmas Coaster

You Will Need:
tin can tops
colored felt
glue
sequins

During the holidays people need lots of coasters to protect their furniture from wet glasses. An easy way to make some as gifts for your family and friends is this:

Choose the top from a tin can big enough to cover the base of a glass. Cut two circles of felt an eighth of an inch larger in diameter than the can top. Cover one entire surface of each felt circle with glue. Insert the can top between the glued surfaces, and press the edges together.

Decorate with felt cutouts and sequins.

Stack several coasters together and tie with ribbon and holly as a gift.

Christmas Lantern

You Will Need:

empty tin can
funnel to fit over can
modeling clay
sharp nail
small hammer
spray paint
votive candle in glass cup
tin snips
block of wood

Fill the can with water and put it where the water will freeze. When it is frozen, put the can on its side, and with the hammer and nail make holes in the can in any design you wish. (The ice provides a firm substance to hammer against). Turn the can until you have made a design all around it. Hold the can under hot water and let the ice melt. Dry the can thoroughly, and paint it with spray paint any color you wish.

With tin snips cut the end of the funnel so that only an inch remains. Place a block of wood inside the funnel, and hammer a design in it as you did in the can. Remove the wood and spray the funnel the same color as the can.

Fasten the glass cup containing the candle inside the can with modeling clay. Place the funnel upside down on top of the can as a lid.

These lanterns make pretty lights for garden or patio tables as well as being attractive for use in the house at Christmas. They make welcome gifts for people who do a lot of outdoor living.

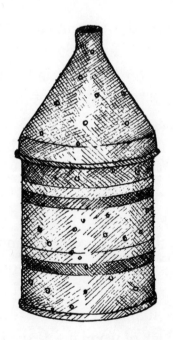

Drum Tree Ornament

You Will Need:
small empty tin can with separate lid
colored felt
narrow gold braid
narrow velvet ribbon
gold cord

To make this ornament in the form of a drum that complements the wooden soldier ornament on page 69, cut colored felt the proper size to cover the outside of the can and glue it on. Cut two circles of felt just enough larger than the top of the can so that you can insert it between them and glue edges together. Then glue it to the top.

Cut a piece of gold cord large enough to loop from one side to the other, and glue the ends to the felt at each side. Glue a strip of gold braid down each side. Crisscross narrow velvet ribbon in the spaces between. Glue gold braid around the top and bottom, covering the ends of the cord and the ribbon.

Ornaments from Plastic Glasses

When you use plastic glasses at picnics or large parties, don't throw them away. Wash and save them for making things at Christmas.

BELL

You Will Need:
plastic glasses
enamel model paint
wire
small colored ball
hatpin or skewer

To make a bell from a plastic glass, paint it with enamel model paint. Carefully heat a hatpin or skewer and make two holes in the center of the bottom of the glass.

Fasten a small colored Christmas tree ball (to represent a clapper) to a wire and holding the glass upside down, thread the wire up through one hole and down through the other. Fasten together on the inside, leaving enough wire outside to form a loop.

You can make a gay door decoration by tying several of these bells together with ribbon and attaching them to a green pine bough.

PARTY GLASSES

Make gay glasses for a holiday party by decorating them with painted holly sprigs. Do this by painting triangles of three red dots at intervals on the glass and paint green holly leaves between the dots.

Winter Doorstop

You Will Need:
plastic bleach or detergent jug
5 cups plaster of paris
2½ cups water
artificial holly
small Santa Claus figure
contact paper
velvet ribbon

A Christmas gift that will keep doors from blowing in winter winds is a holiday doorstop.

Cut off the top of the plastic jug, leaving a five inch base. Mix the plaster with water and fill the base with the mixture. Arrange the artificial material in the plaster. It takes about ten minutes for the plaster to fully harden, so gauge your working time accordingly. Stick the Santa Claus figure in the middle.

Cut contact paper to fit the sides, folding the edges under the bottom. Tie a ribbon around it with a bow in front.

There is another variation of this doorstop that is very pretty, but must be planned well in advance of Christmas. Substitute preserved foliage, silver and gold sprayed seedpods, and dried weeds for the artificial holly.

Holiday Napkin Holder

White, red or green spray can tops make pretty Christmas napkin holders. All you have to do is to remove the round top with shears, leaving a ring.

Tie any decoration on the ring with narrow velvet ribbon. The one shown here uses a yarn candy cane as described on page 77.

Foil Christmas Tree Balls

You Will Need:
newspaper
aluminum foil
metal Christmas Tree ornament hangers

Sometimes there is a very large tree to decorate, perhaps in a schoolroom or auditorium. Here is an easy way to make a great many effective ornaments.

Cut sheets of newspaper into quarters. Crumple them in your hand, molding them into a ball shape. Keep adding newspaper until you have the size ball you want.

Cut aluminum foil into squares large enough to cover the newspaper balls, and mold it around them. The crumpled foil makes the balls look sparkly.

Pry the small end of a metal Christmas ornament hanger open far enough so that it will stick into the ball, and hang it to the tree by the larger end.

Snowflakes

You Will Need:
cardboard or plastic meat containers
 from the supermarket
spray paint

Cardboard or plastic meat containers from the supermarket have different shapes and composition which lend themselves to interesting design. Illustrated here are some patterns we have cut to form snowflakes. Sprayed with gold or silver paint, these can be hung from the tree with a loop of colored thread.

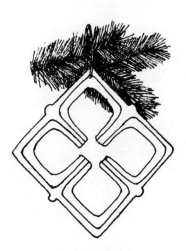

Four-Dimensional Christmas Tree

You Will Need:
shirt cardboard or stiff paper

A table decoration that is easy and inexpensive to make is a modern cardboard tree. Draw and cut out two identical triangular shape trees, forming a wide trunk at the exact middle of the bottom of the triangle. On one tree cut a line up the middle of the trunk to the midpoint of the tree. On the other tree, cut a line down from the top to the midpoint of the tree. Slide one tree over the other and stand. This tree can be painted and decorated with glitter or anything you wish.

Decorations and Gifts from Miscellaneous Materials

In addition to using things from nature and objects that are normally thrown away, you can make many attractive gifts and decorations with inexpensive materials that are readily available.

We have described some of these in the following chapter. We suggest that you build a supply of pieces of ribbon, stones from discarded costume jewelry, beads from broken necklaces, and stray artificial flowers to decorate your gifts.

Sparkle Ball

You Will Need:
a balloon
a ball of heavy cotton string
glue
glitter
vaseline or petroleum jelly

You can use sparkle balls as a basis for decorations. They are fun to make.

Blow up the balloon to the size you want your ball. Dilute a third of a cup of water soluble glue with two table-spoons of water. Measure off several yards of string, and soak it in the glue for about five minutes.

Spread the surface of the balloon lightly with the jelly substance. Wrap the soaked string around the balloon in a crisscross pattern, forming a network. The closer you weave it the stronger it will be. Sprinkle glitter over the string network.

Let the ball dry overnight. Pierce the balloon and draw it through a hole in the network. You now have an open-work sparkling ball.

Sparkle Ball Tree Centerpiece or Mantle Decoration

You Will Need:

materials for basic sparkle ball

a tin can

a quarter-inch dowel

twistums (the fasteners that come with plastic bags)

plaster of paris

silver spray

thumbtack

decorative material to cover can

Make ten sparkle balls about four inches in diameter. Fasten the balls into a tree shape, connecting them with twistums. Use three balls for the bottom of the tree, two for the next layer, and two, one on top of the other, to form the peak.

Mix two parts plaster of paris and one part water. Fill the can with the mixture. Cut dowel to measure from the top of the tree to the bottom of the can and paint it with glue and glitter to match that used on the balls forming the tree. Insert it in the plaster before the plaster hardens. When firm, thread the tree over the dowel and fasten it at the top of the dowel with a thumb-tack to hold it in place.

Cover the can with decorative material. We used a mixture of green and silver glitter for the tree, and a green metallic ribbon at the base that was pierced with holes through which the silver color of the can showed.

Sparkle Ball Hanging Basket for Colored Balls

You Will Need:
materials for basic sparkle ball
about 30 yards of ribbon straw or
   similar material
Christmas tree balls
florist pick
twistums

This is a way to use a sparkle ball to make a gay hanging decoration.

Make the balloon about eight inches in diameter. When you wind the string network leave about two inches of the top of the balloon bare, so that when you remove it there will be a wide opening.

Cut the straw ribbon into one yard strands. Braid three strands together. Using three of these braids make a rope by braiding them together. Do this twice more so that you have three ropes.

Tie these together at one end, fasten one rope to each of three sides of the ball, and bring the ends together again at the bottom. You now have a hanging basket.

64

Make a tassel by winding straw ribbon around a three inch cardboard to the thickness you desire. Remove the cardboard, and tie the bunched ribbon tightly an inch from the top. Cut the bottom loops.

Fasten the tassel to the bottom of the basket in this way. Make a four inch braided rope. Fold it in half and wire a florist pick to it at the bend. Insert the pick down through the center of the tassel. Bring the ends of the rope up through the bottom of the basket and fasten with twistums.

Fill the basket with colored Christmas balls.

Kissing Ball

A sparkle ball makes a beautiful kissing ball.

Make the balloon eight inches in diameter, and finish according to the basic directions, leaving enough space as you wind the string network so that you can eventually insert a sprig of mistletoe through the holes.

You can make a full looking spray by putting several individual sprigs through the holes and wiring them together at the top.

Tie bows to the top and bottom of the ball, and hang it with a long loop of ribbon.

Jewel Tree

You Will Need:
styrofoam cone
small glass Christmas tree balls
glue

Jewel trees are easy to make and most effective Christmas decorations.

Dip the end of a ball including the wire loop into glue and push it into the top of the cone. Repeat, working down from the top until the entire tree is covered.

You can make large or small trees depending on the size of the cone, but remember to use balls that are appropriate in size to the cone.

Personalized Christmas Ball

You Will Need:
a Christmas tree ball
two watercolor paintbrushes
glue
glitter
narrow ribbon

A pretty way to remember a friend at Christmas is to give him or her a personalized Christmas tree ball.

With one brush and glue, paint your friend's name in block letters on the ball. Roll in glitter. With the dry brush remove excess glitter. Make a ribbon bow in the ring at the top of the ball.

PLACE CARD

You can make a very effective place card with one of these balls in this way: cut a half-inch ring from cardboard tubing such as that used in rolls of gift wrapping paper. Cover the ring with foil to match the ball.

The ring will form a little stand so that the ball will remain upright on the table.

68

Wooden Soldier Ornament

You Will Need:
balsa wood or poster board
enamel paint

Boys and girls enjoy making wooden soldier ornaments for a Christmas tree.

Trace the pattern shown here on balsa wood and cut it out with a knife. When the form is cut out, paint it on each side with white enamel. Of course, if you use white poster board you won't have to paint it white.

Draw in the design as shown lightly with pencil, and paint it as you like. The white enamel base coat will be sufficient for the face, hands and breeches.

Make a hole in the top and attach a cord for hanging.

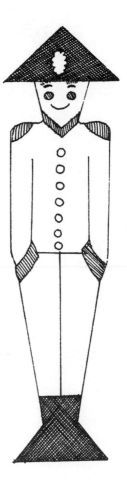

Snow Scene Centerpiece

You Will Need:
a flat board or tray
plaster of paris
twigs and tiny branches to represent
   bare trees
miniature figures which may include
   animals, skaters, sledders, village
   houses, a mirror to simulate a pond
small pieces of evergreen
large pebbles to represent rocks

It is fascinating to make an outdoor
snow scene to use as a Christmas table
centerpiece, to put under a Christmas
tree or as an ornamental conversation
piece. You can make one any size. The
important thing to remember is scale.
Everything must be in proper propor-
tion. Figures must relate to each other
in size, and to the trees, rocks, bushes
or whatever else you use as background.

Place the foundation board or tray on
a piece of foil to protect the work area
from spilled plaster. Fasten twigs that
represent trees, evergreen pieces for

pine trees and low bushes to the foundation board with modeling clay. Put "rocks" where desired to vary the landscape. You can use lumps of crumpled wet newspaper to make different ground levels.

When the landscape parts are in place mix plaster of paris with water until it is the consistency of thick whipped cream. Spoon it over the board and around the base of the trees, covering the newspaper. It is interesting to leave some of the surface of the rocks exposed. If you are using a mirror for a pond, press it into the surface of the plaster. You have about ten minutes to work with the plaster before it hardens.

Glue any figure you are using to the mirror (skaters, sled) or to the hardened surface.

Place Mat Case

You Will Need:
a sheet of acetate 25x20 inches (pur-
    chased at a stationery store)
a sheet of poster board
a punch
ribbon, yarn, straw ribbon or raffia

Any housekeeper who has had to cope
with rumpled doilies and place mats
will welcome one or more of these
pretty cases as a Christmas gift.

Cut the acetate in half. Holding the
two pieces together, punch holes along
the top and two sides at three-quarter
inch intervals. Wind the ribbon material
through the holes, starting at the top
of one side. Finish the ends with a little
bow.

After you've ironed
Every mat,
This little case
Will keep them flat

Cut a piece of poster board on which to place the mats to fit the opening, making sure that it will slide in easily. Round the corners of the acetate case and the poster board.

It might be fun to write the following jingle on a plain white file card, decorate the card in a holly design with paint or marking pens and slip it inside the case.

After you've ironed
Every mat
This little case
Will keep them flat.

Christmas Napkin Holders

You Will Need:
cookie cutters
clip clothespins
felt
glue
assorted decorations

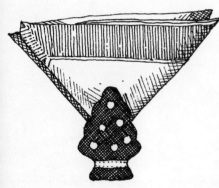

Use clip clothespins to make gay napkin holders.

Trace the shape of a Christmas tree on green felt. Be sure that it is large enough to cover a clip clothespin. Use your imagination to decorate the felt tree. You can use little shapes cut from colored felt, beads, sequins, tiny shells —in fact anything that appeals to you.

When you have decorated the tree, glue it to the clothespin with the base of the tree at the open end. Clip a folded paper napkin into the other end.

These napkin holders are effective when you use them with the tree place cards described on page 44. You can use the same cookie cutter to trace the shape so that they match.

Christmas Bobèche

You Will Need:

⅛ inch mesh hardware cloth (this is metal screening you can buy at a hardware store)

heavy shears

tiny colored Christmas tree balls

Bobèche is a French word meaning candle ring. It is pronounced *bow-besh*.

We like to use as many candles and candlesticks as possible at Christmas time, and bobèches add to their festive appearance.

Cut the shape as shown in the pattern from the hardware cloth with heavy shears. Fasten balls in the color

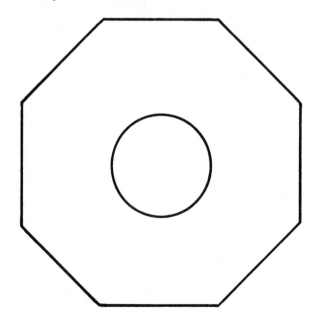

you wish by removing the metal prongs from the top of the base, sticking one prong through an opening in the mesh, and pushing both back in the ball. Put the bobèche on top of the candlestick and insert the candle through the hole in the center of the bobèche.

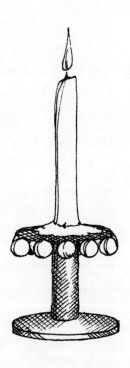

Yarn Candy Canes

You Will Need:
large spool
four small headed nails
red and white yarn
a knitting needle, crochet hook or other
   pointed instrument
needle and thread

Many people have had fun making horse reins with a knitting spool. This is a way to use one to make candy cane shapes for Christmas decorations.

Drive the four nails into the top of the spool making a square. Leave half an inch of the nail showing.

Push about seven inches of the white yarn down through the hole in the top of the spool. This is the tail.

Place the yarn you are working with on the left side of the left hand nail, and bring it around working counterclockwise. Again working counterclockwise loop the yarn around the other nails.

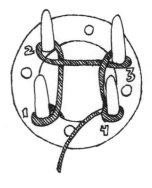

Put the yarn across the front of the first nail above the original loop. Put the knitting needle or crochet hook into the original bottom loop. Pick it up and

slip it over the top piece of yarn until it drops off the nail. Pull the tail hanging through the spool to make an even stitch.

Turn the spool counterclockwise until the next nail is in front of you, and do the same on it. Continue in this manner with the other nails, pulling the tail after each stitch.

When you have made about an inch of tubing with the white yarn, hold it aside and push a seven inch piece of red yarn down through the hole in the spool as you did the white. Now work for an inch with the red yarn. Continue alternating white and red until you have a long length of tubing.

Cut the tubing straight across every five inches. As you pull away the pieces of cut loop, you will see that whole loops are left. Pull these together at each end with a needle and thread.

Force a piece of firm wire up the center of the tubing, and bend into candy cane shape.

Use these yarn canes on the tree or as package decorations. You can also leave the tubing uncut and use it as a garland on the tree.

Things to Do
With Christmas Cards

Do save Christmas cards from one year to another. You can use them in many ways.

CHRISTMAS PACKAGES

To make a Christmas package decorative in an unusual way, select a Christmas card the right size to cover most of the top of the box you are wrapping. Choose a solid color paper that will complement the main color in the Christmas card for a wrapping. Paste the card on top. With the colored paper framing the card it isn't necessary to add ribbon or other decorations to have a beautiful package.

Even more fun is to choose a card that is personally appropriate for the recipient of the gift you are wrapping—a nautical Santa Claus for a boating uncle, small animals grouped around a woodland Christmas tree for a young friend or a scene of Santa's workshop for a wood working father. You will be surprised how many times there is just the right card to use.

TAGS FOR PACKAGES

Cutting figures from Christmas cards is a way to insure having plenty of tags for Christmas packages. They are colorful and amusing. A stunning tag can be made by cutting out a Christmas greeting that is embossed on heavy paper. Punch a hole in the top and insert a loop of gold, silver, red or green cord.

MATCHBOX GIFTS

You can cut scenes from small cards, or small scale motifs from larger ones to fit the sides of small matchboxes. These are gay accessories to use during the Christmas season. Or you can put several in a cellophane bag, tie it with red ribbon and holly and deliver it as a "more than a card, less than a gift" remembrance to a neighbor.

CHRISTMAS CARDS

You can make your own Christmas cards by cutting pictures from used cards and pasting them on construction paper. Cut the paper large enough to frame the picture, leaving room to write your message on the bottom.

When you make your cards this way you can have the fun of choosing a picture that is especially appropriate for the person to whom you are sending it.

Christmas Goodies

Christmas is a time of holiday parties and festive family dinners. Almost everyone has favorite foods that they serve at this time. In this chapter we are sharing some of ours with you.

Christmas Cookies

One of the things that is most fun to do at Christmas time is to bake and decorate cookies, either to serve, give as gifts, or use as tree decorations. Here is an easy recipe.

1 cup sugar
4 T. butter or margarine
1 egg
3 T. milk
2 heaping cups flour
1 t. any baking powder
1 t. vanilla
pinch salt

Soften butter. Stir in sugar until well mixed. Add egg unbeaten. Mix well into butter and sugar mixture.

Add vanilla and salt to milk.

Sift flour with baking powder.

Add flour and milk alternately, a little at a time, to first mixture and beat well.

Chill the dough until it is very firm. Roll it between sheets of waxed paper to a thickness of one eighth inch. Cut into shapes with cookie cutter. Bake on a greased cookie sheet in a 325° oven for 8-10 minutes.

If you want to use the cookies as tree decorations, make a hole in each with a piece of toothpick or matchstick before you bake them. Leave the stick in while baking so the hole doesn't close. Then when the cookies are done you can hang them on the tree.

To decorate the cookies you can use:

colored sugar
nut meats
small candies
chocolate sprinkles
raisins
currants
candied cherries

There are many things that are fun to do. You can make holly berries and leaves or poinsettia flowers with pieces of red and green candied cherries. You can make happy faces with raisins and currants for eyes and nose and red cherry pieces for lips. You can sprinkle green sugar on a Christmas tree shape and decorate it with tiny candies like cinnamon drops and the ones you can buy in most grocery shops that look like little silver balls.

To package cookies as gifts you can paint cans like coffee or nut cans that have separate plastic tops. Or you might use the plastic trays in which things are packaged in the supermarkets, and cover them with colored cellophane.

Gingerbread Men

Recipe:

Preheat oven to 350 degrees
Blend until creamy:
   ¼ cup butter
   ½ cup white or brown sugar
Beat in:
   ½ cup dark molasses
Sift:
   3½ cups all purpose flour
Resift with:
   1 t. soda
   ¼ t. cloves
   ½ t. cinnamon
   1 t. ginger
   ½ t. salt

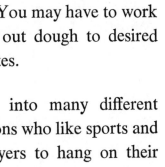

Icing

1½ cups confectioners sugar
2 T. hot milk
1½ t. butter
½ t. vanilla

Add the sifted ingredients to the butter mixture in about 3 parts alternating with ¼ cup water. You may have to work the flour in with your hands. Roll out dough to desired thickness. Cut. Bake for 8-10 minutes.

Gingerbread men can be made into many different shapes. One of our friends has two sons who like sports and they made gingerbread hockey players to hang on their tree. Use your imagination to decorate your own.

Turkish Delight Candy

Our Christmas is not complete without a candy called Turkish Delight. It is delicious, easy to make, and the red and green squares, packed in a decorated tin make a welcome gift.

This is the recipe:

3 ½ T. gelatin
¾ cup cold water
1 ½ cups boiling fruit juice*
3 cups sugar
2 T. lemon juice
grated rind of one lemon
red or green coloring
confectioners sugar

Soak the gelatin in the cold water.
Pour boiling fruit juice (either orange juice or a canned mixed juice) over the sugar.
Stir over a low flame until sugar is dissolved.
Add soaked gelatin and grated lemon rind.
Bring to boiling point and boil for ten minutes.
Add lemon juice and red coloring.
Pour into six inch square pan that has been dipped in cold water.
Let harden for twelve hours.
Cut into squares with a knife dipped in hot water.

Roll each square in confectioners sugar.
Omit lemon juice and rind.
Flavor with peppermint.
Color green.

* For a variation of recipe use boiling water instead of fruit
  juice.

Orange Dessert

The orange is a fruit that has been associated with Christmas for many, many years. Countless children have known that the big lump in the toe of their Christmas stockings would turn out to be an orange.

This is a dessert, using an orange, that is light and delicious, and perhaps more welcome after a tremendous Christmas dinner than some of the richer traditional ones.

Select oranges of uniform size and bright color. Cut off the top third. Remove the pulp and juice. Put this aside to use at another time in a fruit cup or other dessert.

Fill the hollow orange with lemon, lime or pineapple ice.

Keep in the freezer until ready to serve. At that time decorate the top with mint leaves and small pieces of candied fruit.

Delicious and Pretty

When this dessert was introduced into our family many years ago it didn't have a name, but people said "It's delicious and pretty," so that is the name we've always called it by. It is particularly festive looking at Christmas. For a quart mold you will need two boxes of frozen raspberries or strawberries and a pint of heavy cream, a tablespoon of sugar and vanilla flavoring.

Puree the berries and put in bottom of a mold. Whip cream, flavor with vanilla, and spoon on top of berry puree. Cover with foil and put in freezer.

At serving time unmold and put on serving plate. To unmold it, cut around edge of mold with a knife. Hold in bowl of hot water while you count three slowly. Then invert onto plate. Juice from the berries runs down the sides of the mold making a pretty red and white appearance. Surround the mold with sprigs of holly.

We have found that it is convenient to make the mold in advance of when you want to use it. Then you can unmold it at a convenient time, wrap it well in foil and replace it in the freezer.

Snowball Dessert

This is a dessert that you can make well in advance of the holidays.

With a scoop make individual balls of ice cream and put them on a foil covered cookie sheet or tray. Sprinkle them thoroughly with coconut. Put more foil over the top and keep them in a freezer until ready to use.

At serving time, when you place them on a plate, decorate them with a sprig of holly if they are to be served during the day. At night insert a lighted red birthday candle in the top of the base for a gay decoration.

To make this dessert even more delicious, pass chocolate sauce to pour over the snowballs.

Holiday Dessert

This holiday dessert looks like a tiny pot of holly and causes exclamations of delight when it is served.

To make it you will need:

3 inch flower pots
foil
ice cream
chocolate wafers or chocolate sprinkles
straws
sprigs of holly

Line the flower pots with foil. Roll chocolate wafers into fine crumbs or powder them in a blender. Put a layer of crumbs or chocolate sprinkles in the bottom of a pot. Fill it with ice cream. Cover the top of the ice cream with more chocolate crumbs or sprinkles.

Cut a straw the height of the pot, and insert it in the ice cream. Put a three or four inch sprig of real or artificial holly in the straw.

Popcorn Bowl

Children in our neighborhood love to visit one particular house at Christmas time, for on the hall table is a big silver bowl of popcorn balls wrapped in green, red and silver foil. Everyone is welcome to help themselves, and the bowl is constantly refilled.

This is the way you can make popcorn balls and have a welcome bowl in your own house.

Melt 1 ½ t. butter

Stir into it:

   ½ cup molasses

   ¼ cup sugar

Mix until sugar is dissolved.

Boil (but don't stir) this mixture until a bit of the syrup dropped from the end of a spoon forms a hard ball in cold water.

Stir six cups of popped corn into the syrup until all the kernels are covered.

When this is cool, form it into balls.

Wrap each ball in colored foil.

Birds' Christmas Tree

When we are planning our holiday feasts it is nice to think of the birds and plan a feast for them too.

You can do this by making a Christmas banquet tree for birds. Either use a small evergreen tree growing in your yard, or buy a leftover tree after Christmas. The birds won't know if their feast comes on the proper day.

Make a star for the top from a piece of heavy cardboard, and cover it thickly on each side with peanut butter. Stick fat white popcorn kernels in the peanut butter until the star is solidly white.

Save the hollow halves of grapefruit and oranges and fill them with a mixture of bacon fat, breadcrumbs and bird seed. Attach colored ribbon, yarn or raffia handles and hang them on the tree.

Stick colorful sprays of berries like pyracantha (firethorn), bayberry and holly in the green branches, and garland the tree with cranberries strung on heavy thread.

If you live in an apartment, you can make a miniature tree for the birds that they will love, and put it on your outside windowsill. Get a large pine cone with open petals. Most florists sell these at Christmas time. Save things like bread and cracker crumbs, leftover cereal, broken nuts, melon seeds, and broken potato chips and stir them into melted suet and bacon fat. When the mixture hardens, fill the crevices between the petals of the cone with it.

Index